The eyes of the LORD are on the righteous, and *his ears are attentive* to their cry.

PSALM 34:15

_____

_____

_____

_____

_____

_____

_____

_____

_____

_____

_____

_____

_____

_____

_____

_____

_____

_____

_____

_____

I sought the LORD, *and he answered me*;

he delivered me from all my fears.

PSALM 34:4

God is still good, even when circumstances are not.

Marlena

In times of change, God invites us to wrap ourselves
in His presence and trust in His purposes.

The Lord gives strength to his people;
the LORD blesses his people with peace.

PSALM 29:11

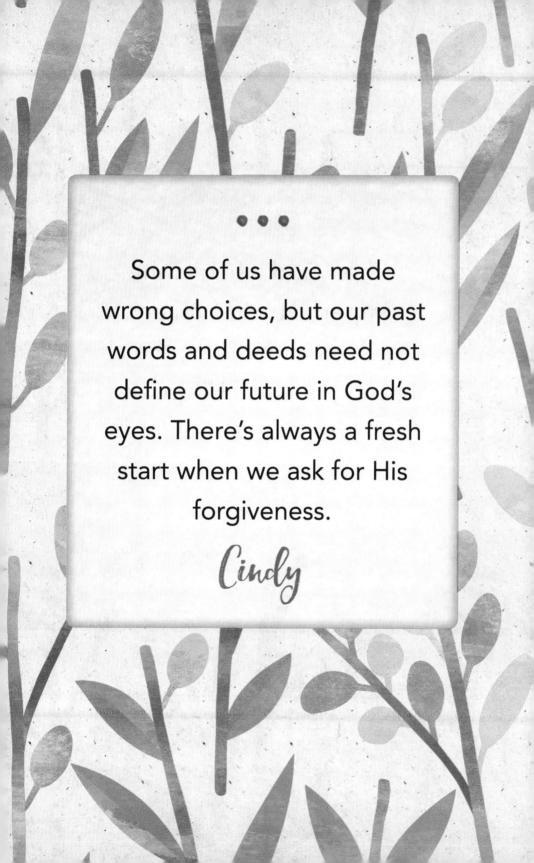

• • •

Some of us have made wrong choices, but our past words and deeds need not define our future in God's eyes. There's always a fresh start when we ask for His forgiveness.

Cindy

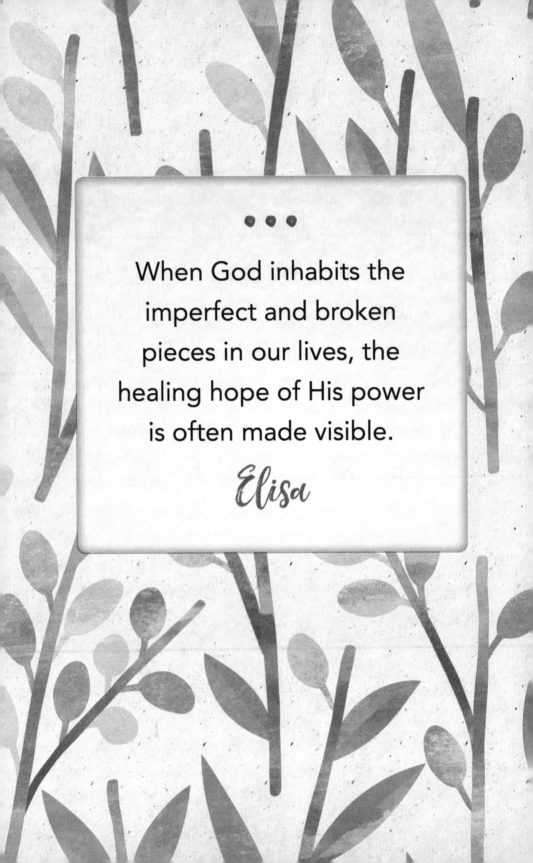

• • •

When God inhabits the imperfect and broken pieces in our lives, the healing hope of His power is often made visible.

Elisa

The LORD delights in those who fear him,
who put their hope in *his unfailing love*.

PSALM 147:11

We have a God who understands that we grow weary, and
He invites us to cast our burdens on Him.

"*Never will I leave you*; never will I forsake you."

HEBREWS 13:5

God made our hearts, and He understands everything we do.

He has the power to intervene in our lives and deliver us.

Poh Fang

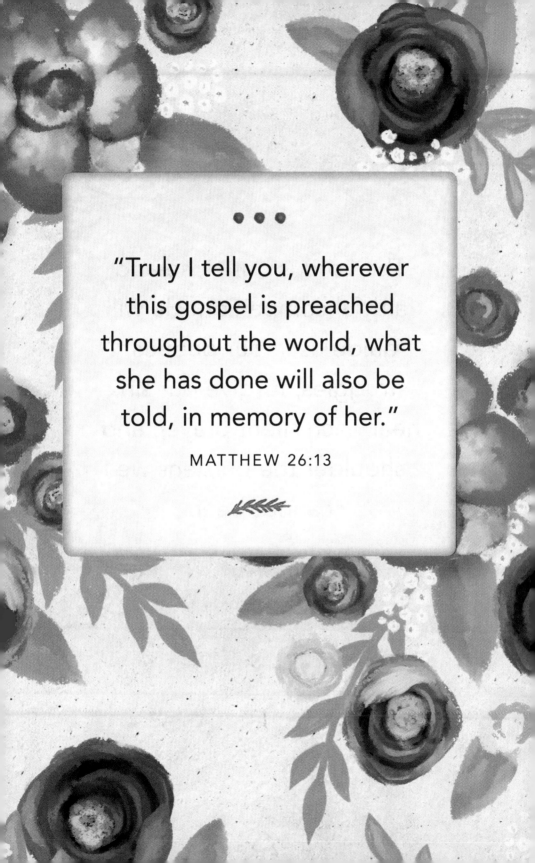

"Truly I tell you, wherever this gospel is preached throughout the world, what she has done will also be told, in memory of her."

MATTHEW 26:13

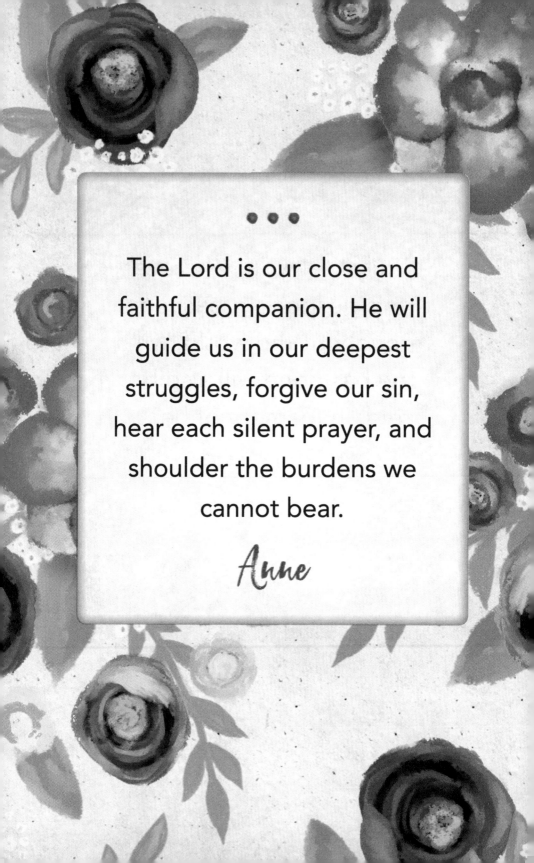

• • •

The Lord is our close and faithful companion. He will guide us in our deepest struggles, forgive our sin, hear each silent prayer, and shoulder the burdens we cannot bear.

Anne

No one is hopeless and beyond God's saving help.
We have a King who can put people back together again.

Joanie

"Let your *light shine* before others, that they may see
your good deeds and glorify your Father in heaven."

MATTHEW 5:16

There is peace in knowing that whatever we do and wherever we go, we go with God, who promised never to leave or forsake His followers.

Jennifer

God reaches out to us in our deepest moments of need
and cups us in His hand.

Regina

• • •

Let us then approach
God's throne of grace with
confidence, so that we may
receive mercy and
find grace to help us in
our time of need.

HEBREWS 4:16

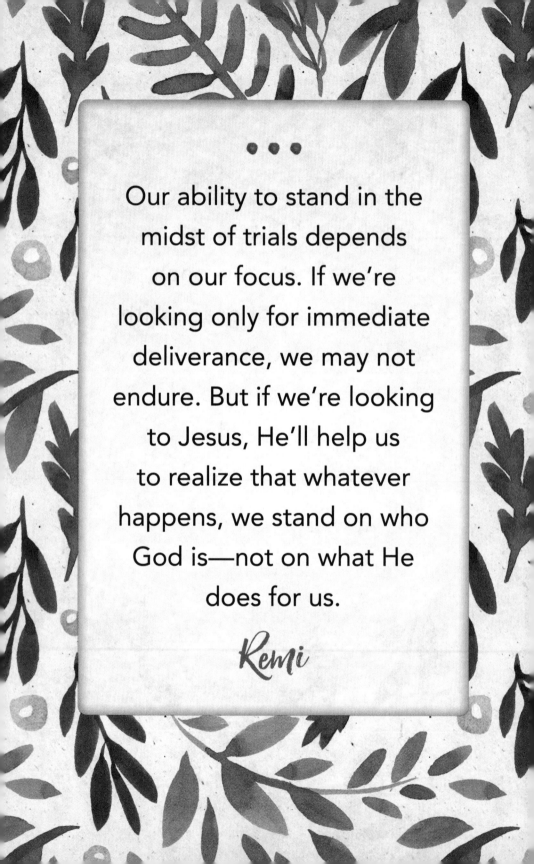

Our ability to stand in the midst of trials depends on our focus. If we're looking only for immediate deliverance, we may not endure. But if we're looking to Jesus, He'll help us to realize that whatever happens, we stand on who God is—not on what He does for us.

Remi

Give thanks to the LORD, for he is good; his *love endures* forever.

PSALM 106:1

Cast your cares on the LORD and he will sustain you;
he will never let the righteous be shaken.

PSALM 55:22

Life's pleasures can't compare to the blessings of God.

Marlena

....
....
....
....
....
....
....
....
....
....
....
....
....
....
....
....
....
....
....
....
....

When *the Lord saw her*, his heart went out
to her and he said, "Don't cry."

LUKE 7:13

• • •

This is how God showed
his love among us: He sent
his one and only Son into
the world that we might
live through him.

1 JOHN 4:9

• • •

We need each other; we
all have burdens to bear.
Let's use the strength
Christ gives us to minister
to others and find ways to
lighten their load.

Joanie

Are you being tested today? Remember, there are many promises in the Bible. Generations have proven them true, and so can you.

Joanie

_____

_____

_____

_____

_____

_____

_____

_____

_____

_____

_____

_____

_____

_____

_____

_____

_____

_____

_____

_____

_____

_____

When our lives reflect the reality of God's love,
we leave a lasting legacy for others.

Keila

How amazing that the great God who created the world
in all its splendor cares for you and me!

Alyson

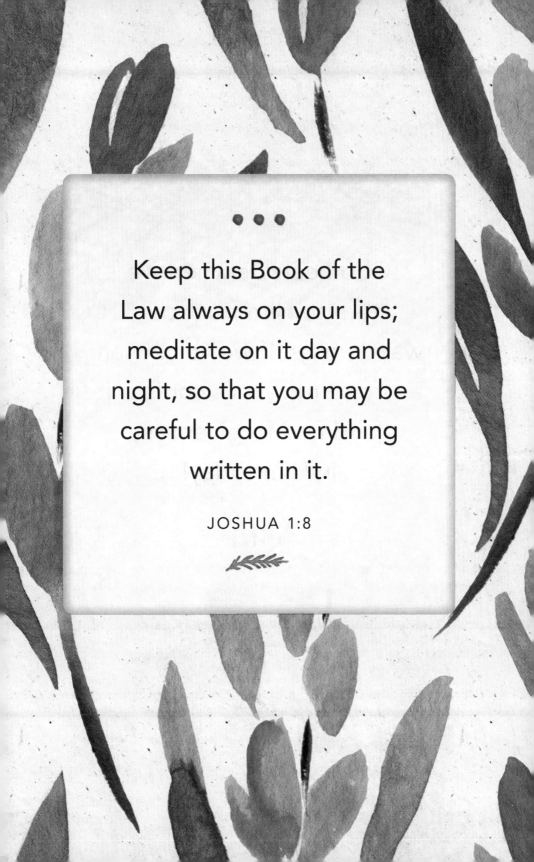

Keep this Book of the Law always on your lips; meditate on it day and night, so that you may be careful to do everything written in it.

JOSHUA 1:8

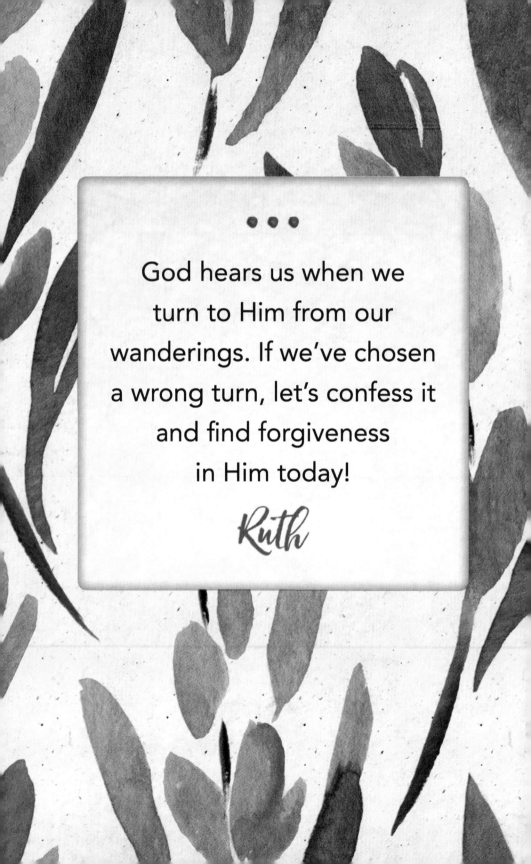

• • •

God hears us when we
turn to Him from our
wanderings. If we've chosen
a wrong turn, let's confess it
and find forgiveness
in Him today!

Ruth

"*Come to me*, all you who are weary and
burdened, and I will give you rest."

MATTHEW 11:28

When we remember who God is and how much
He loves us, we can relax into His peace.

Keila

Pour out your hearts to him, for *God is our refuge.*

PSALM 62:8

_____
_____
_____
_____
_____
_____
_____
_____
_____
_____
_____
_____
_____
_____
_____
_____
_____
_____
_____
_____
_____
_____
_____
_____

Prayer is a conversation with God, not a formula. Just talk with
your Father. He wants to hear what's on your heart.

Anne

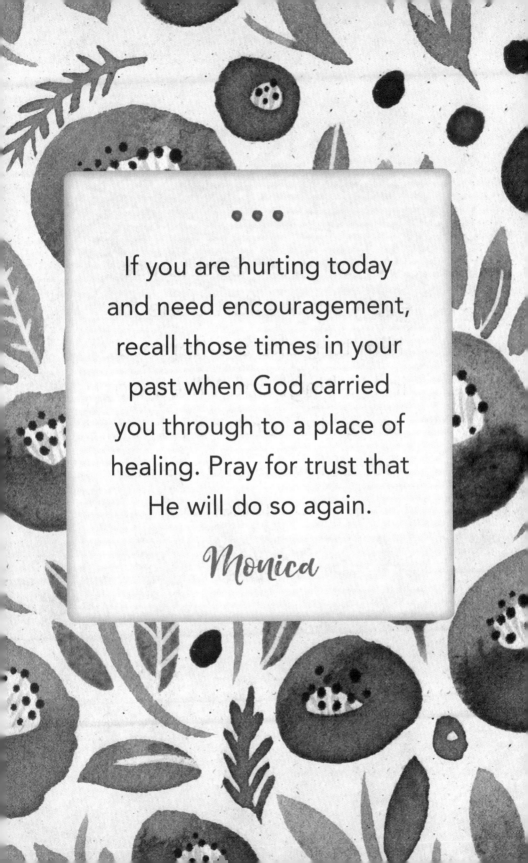

If you are hurting today
and need encouragement,
recall those times in your
past when God carried
you through to a place of
healing. Pray for trust that
He will do so again.

Monica

We can trust God to use every small effort done for Him to make a difference in His kingdom. When we serve the Lord, no job or act of love is too menial to matter.

Xochitl

Open my eyes that I may see wonderful things in your law.

PSALM 119:18

Some of our hardest struggles are those deep desires that go unmet.

Keep praying. In His time, God will answer.

Anne

"I have come that *they may have life*, and have it to the full."

JOHN 10:10

We were made to be victorious through the salvation Jesus provided.
We don't have to live in fear. Fear melts before God's love and power!

Regina

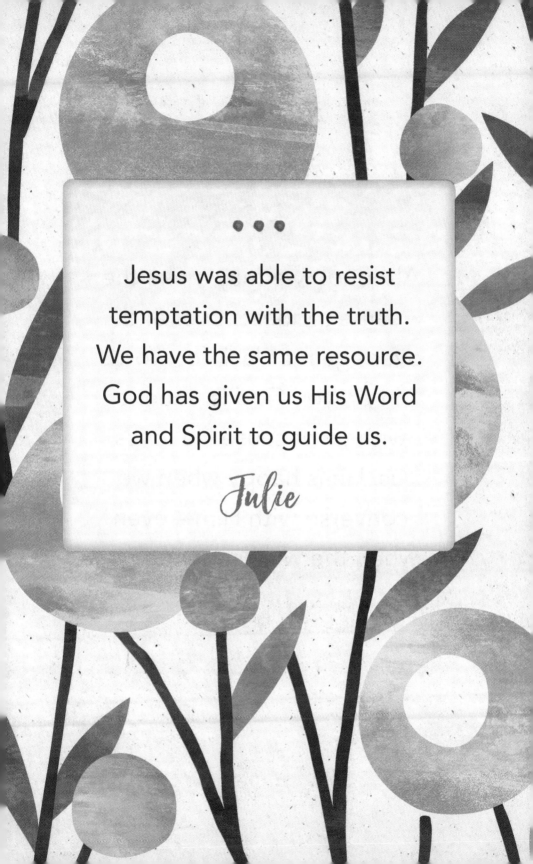

Jesus was able to resist temptation with the truth. We have the same resource. God has given us His Word and Spirit to guide us.

Julie

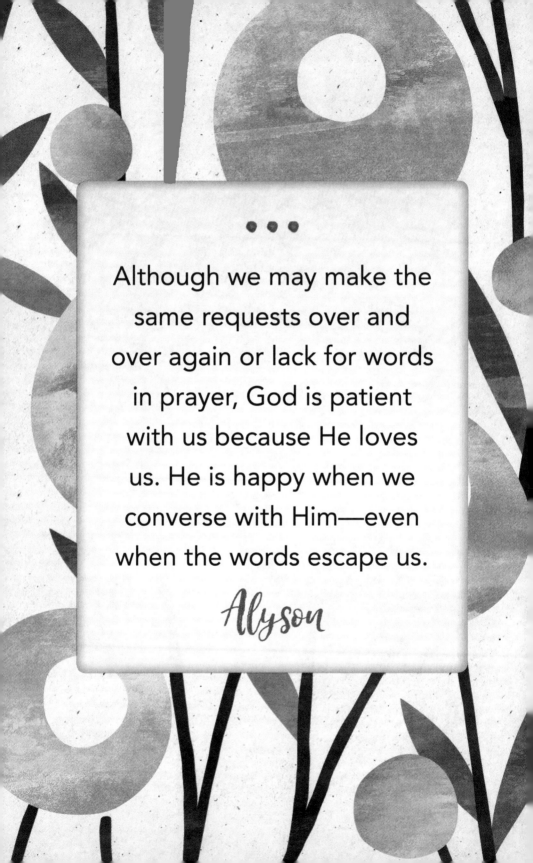

Although we may make the same requests over and over again or lack for words in prayer, God is patient with us because He loves us. He is happy when we converse with Him—even when the words escape us.

Alyson

When God seems silent, it's time for us to wait and trust Him
to sort things out in a way we never could.

Remi

I have hidden your word *in my heart*

that I might not sin against you.

PSALM 119:11

God's grace and love come from a bottomless reservoir.
Drink from the water He offers. You'll never thirst again.

Cindy

"A new command I give you: *Love one another.*
As I have loved you, so you must love one another."

JOHN 13:34

The Writers of *Our Daily Bread*

Alyson Kieda has been an editor for Our Daily Bread Ministries for over a decade and has more than thirty-five years of editing experience. She is married with three adult children and a growing number of grandchildren.

Amy Boucher Pye is a writer, editor, and speaker. The author of *Finding Myself in Britain: Our Search for Faith, Home, and True Identity*, she runs the Woman Alive book club in the UK and enjoys life with her family in their English vicarage.

Anne Cetas began writing for *Our Daily Bread* in September 2004 and is senior content editor for the publication. Anne and her husband, Carl, enjoy walking and bicycling together, and working as mentors in an urban ministry.

Cindy Hess Kasper has served for more than forty years at Our Daily Bread Ministries. Cindy and her husband, Tom, have three grown children and seven grandchildren, in whom they take great delight.

Elisa Morgan has authored over fifteen books on mothering, spiritual formation, and evangelism and blogs at elisamorgan.com. For twenty years, Elisa served as CEO of MOPS International. Elisa is married to Evan, and they have two grown children and two grandchildren who live near them in Denver, Colorado.

Jennifer Benson Schuldt has been writing professionally since 1997 when she graduated from Cedarville University and began her career as a technical writer. Jennifer lives in the Chicago suburbs with her husband, Bob, and their two children.

Joanie Yoder, a favorite among *Our Daily Bread* readers, went home to be with her Savior in 2004. She and her husband established a Christian rehabilitation center for drug addicts in England many years ago. Widowed in 1982, she learned to rely on the Lord's help and strength.

Julie Ackerman Link, after a battle with cancer, went to be with the Lord on April 10, 2015. Julie began writing articles each month for *Our Daily Bread* in 2000. Julie wrote the books *Above All, Love* and *100 Prayers Inspired by the Psalms*.

Karen Wolfe is a native of Jamaica who now lives in the US. She became a follower of Christ at age twenty-six, and one of the first devotionals she read was *Our Daily Bread*. She completed her biblical studies degree at New Orleans Baptist Theological Seminary. She and her husband, Joey, live in Georgia. Karen currently writes at thekarenwolfe.com.

Keila Ochoa and her husband have two young children. She helps Media Associates International with their training ministry for writers around the world and has written several books in Spanish for children, teens, and women.

Marion Stroud went to be with her Savior on August 8, 2015, after a battle with cancer. In 2014 Marion began writing for *Our Daily Bread*. She authored two books of prayers, *Dear God, It's Me and It's Urgent* and *It's Just You and Me, Lord*. Marion worked as a cross-cultural trainer for Media Associates International, helping writers produce books for their own culture. Marion is survived by her husband, Gordon, and their five children and sixteen grandchildren.

Marlena Graves is a bylined contributor for Her.meneutics, Gifted For Leadership, and Missio Alliance. She authored *A Beautiful Disaster: Finding Hope in the Midst of Brokenness*. She and her husband, Shawn, have three girls.

Monica Brands studied English and theology at Trinity Christian College and worked with children with special needs at Elim Christian Services before completing a master of theological studies degree at Calvin Seminary. She now edits for Our Daily Bread Ministries.

Poh Fang Chia is director of content development with Our Daily Bread Ministries at the Singapore office and is also a member of the Chinese editorial review committee.

Regina Franklin is a teacher and freelance writer, and serves alongside her pastor-husband in ministry. She and Scott have two children, Charis and Micah.

Remi Oyedele is a finance professional and freelance writer with twin passions for God's Word and children's books. She blogs at wordzpread.com. A native of Nigeria, she currently resides in Central Florida with her husband, David.

Roxanne Robbins is a former sports reporter, public relations specialist, and Olympic chaplain. She left it all behind to move to East Africa. Now based in Florida, Roxanne directs a nonprofit organization she founded to provide resources and opportunities for orphaned and vulnerable children in Uganda.

Ruth O'Reilly-Smith is a secondary school teacher with twenty years of radio broadcasting experience in South Africa and the UK. Ruth is married to an Englishman, and they have been blessed with twins.

Xochitl (soh-cheel) Dixon is an author, speaker, and blogger at xedixon.com. She enjoys singing, reading, photography, motherhood, and being married to her best friend, Dr. W. Alan Dixon Sr.

God Hears Her Journal

© 2018 by Discovery House

All rights reserved.

Discovery House is affiliated with Our Daily Bread Ministries, Grand Rapids, Michigan.

Requests for permission to quote from this book should be directed to: Permissions Department, Discovery House, PO Box 3566, Grand Rapids, MI 49501, or contact us by email at permissionsdept@dhp.org.

Interior design by Gayle Raymer

Image credits: Shutterstock

ISBN: 978-1-62707-914-3

Printed in the United States of America
First printing in 2018